TOWARDS FULL PRESENCE

A PASTORAL REFLECTION ON ENGAGEMENT WITH SOCIAL MEDIA

DICASTERY FOR COMMUNICATION

Our Sunday Visitor
Huntington, Indiana

28 27 26 25 24 23 1 2 3 4 5 6 7 8 9

Our Sunday Visitor Publishing Division, Our Sunday Visitor, Inc., 200 Noll Plaza, Huntington, IN 46750; 1-800-348-2440.

ISBN: 978-1-63966-182-4 (Inventory No. T2883)

eISBN: 978-1-63966-183-1

Cover design: Tyler Ottinger

Cover art: AdobeStock

Interior design: Amanda Falk

Printed in the United States of America

1. Great strides have been made in the digital age, but one of the pressing issues yet to be addressed is how we, as individuals and as an ecclesial community, are to live in the digital world as "loving neighbors" who are genuinely present and attentive to each other on our common journey along the "digital highways."

Advancements in technology have made new kinds of human interactions possible. In fact, the question is no longer whether to engage with the digital world, but how. Social media in particular is an environment where people interact, share experiences, and cultivate relationships unlike ever before. At the same time, however, as communication is increasingly influenced by artificial intelligence, there arises the need to rediscover the human encounter at its very core. Over the last two decades, our relationship with digital platforms has undergone an irreversible transformation. An awareness has emerged that these platforms can evolve to become cocreated spaces, not just something that we passively use. Young people — as well as older generations — are asking to be met where they are, including on social media, because the digital world is "a significant part of young people's identity and way of life."[1]

2. Many Christians are asking for inspiration and guidance since social media, which is one expression of digital culture, has had a profound impact on both our faith communities and our individual spiritual journeys.

Examples of faithful and creative engagement on social media abound around the world, from both local communities as well as individuals who give witness to their faith on these platforms, oftentimes more pervasively than the institutional Church. There are also numerous pastoral and educational initiatives developed by local Churches, movements, communities, congregations, universities, and individuals.

3. The universal Church has also addressed the digital reality. Since 1967, for example, the yearly World Communications Day messages have offered an ongoing reflection on the topic. Beginning in the 1990s these messages addressed the use of the computer, and since the early 2000s they have consistently reflected on aspects of digital culture and social communication. Raising fundamental questions for digital culture, Pope Benedict XVI, in 2009, addressed the shifts in patterns of communication, saying that media should not only foster connections between people but also encourage them to commit themselves to relationships that promote "a culture of respect, dialogue, and friendship."[2] Subsequently, the Church consolidated the image of social media as "spaces," not only "tools," and called for the Good News to be proclaimed also in digital environments.[3] For his part, Pope Francis has acknowledged that the digital world is "indistinguishable from the sphere of everyday life," and it is changing the way humanity accumulates knowledge, disseminates information, and develops relationships.[4]

4. In addition to these reflections, the Church's practical engagement with social media has also been effective.[5] One recent moment clearly demonstrated that digital media is a powerful tool for the Church's ministry. On March 27, 2020, while still in the early stages of the COVID-19 pandemic, Saint Peter's Square was empty but full of presence. A tele-

vised and livestreamed transmission allowed Pope Francis to lead a transformative global experience: a prayer and message addressed to a world in lockdown. In the midst of a health crisis that took the lives of millions, people around the world, quarantined and in isolation, found themselves profoundly united with each other and with the successor of Peter.[6]

Through traditional media and digital technology, the Pope's prayer reached the homes and touched the lives of people all over the world. The open arms of Bernini's colonnade around the square were able to extend an embrace to millions. Though physically distant from each other, those who joined the Pope in that hour were present to one another and could experience a moment of unity and communion.

• • •

5. The following pages are the result of a reflection involving experts, teachers, young professionals and leaders, lay persons, clergy, and religious. The aim is to address some of the main questions involving how Christians should engage social media. They are not meant to be precise "guidelines" for pastoral ministry in this area. The hope, instead, is to promote a common reflection about our digital experiences, encouraging both individuals and communities to take a creative and constructive approach that can foster a culture of neighborliness.

The challenge of fostering peaceful, meaningful, and caring relationships on social media prompts a discussion in academic and professional circles, as well as in ecclesial ones. What kind of humanity is reflected in our presence in digital environments? How much of our digital relationships is the fruit of deep and truthful communication, and how much is merely shaped by unquestioned opinions and passionate reactions? How much of our faith finds living and refreshing digital expressions? And who is my "neighbor" on social media?

• • •

6. The parable of the good Samaritan,[7] by which Jesus makes us answer the question "Who is my neighbor?" is prompted by the question of an expert in the law. "What must I do to *inherit* eternal life?" he asks. The verb "to inherit" reminds us of the *heritage* of the promised land, which is not so much a geographical territory but a symbol of something more profound and lasting, something that every generation has to rediscover and that can help us to reimagine our role within the digital world.

I. WATCHING OUT FOR PITFALLS ON THE DIGITAL HIGHWAYS

Learning to see from the perspective of the one who fell into the hands of robbers (cf. Lk 10:36).

A PROMISED LAND TO REDISCOVER?

7. Social media is only one branch of the much broader and more complex phenomenon of *digitization*, which is the process of transferring many tasks and dimensions of human life to digital platforms. Digital technologies can increase our efficiency, boost our economy, and help us solve previously insurmountable problems. The digital revolution extended our access to information and our ability to connect with one another beyond the limitations of physical space. A process that was already taking place over the past three decades was accelerated by the pandemic. Activities, such as education and work, that were normally carried out in person can now be done at a distance. Countries also made significant changes in their legal and legislative systems, adopting online sessions and voting as an alternative to meeting in person. The rapid pace with which information spreads is also changing how politics operate.

8. With the advent of Web 5.0 and other communication advances, the role of artificial intelligence in the years to come will increasingly impact our experience of reality. We

are witnessing the development of machines that work and make decisions for us, that can learn and predict our behaviors; sensors on our skin that can measure our emotions; machines that answer our questions and learn from our answers, or that use the registers of irony and speak with the voice and expressions of those who are no longer with us. In this ever evolving reality, many questions remain to be answered.[8]

9. The remarkable changes that the world has experienced since the emergence of the internet have also prompted new tensions. Some were born into this culture and are "digital natives"; others are still trying to get used to it as "digital immigrants." In any case, our culture is now a digital culture. To overcome the old dichotomy between "digital" versus "face to face," some no longer speak of "online" versus "offline" but only of "*onlife*," incorporating human and social life in its various expressions, be they in digital or physical spaces.

10. In the context of integrated communication, consisting of the convergence of communication processes, social media plays a decisive role as a forum in which our values, beliefs, language, and assumptions about daily life are shaped. Moreover, for many people, especially those in developing countries, the only contact with digital communication is through social media. Well beyond the act of *using* social media as a tool, we are *living* in an ecosystem shaped at its core by the experience of social sharing. While we still *use* the web to search for information or entertainment, we turn to social media for a sense of belonging and affirmation, transforming it into a vital space where the com-

munication of core values and beliefs takes place.

In this ecosystem, people are asked to trust in the authenticity of the mission statements of social media companies, which promise, for example, to bring the world closer together, to give everyone the power to create and share ideas, or to give everyone a voice. Although we are conscious of the fact that these advertising slogans are almost never put into practice since companies are much more concerned with their profits, we still tend to believe the promises.

11. Indeed, when people began to utilize the internet a few decades ago, they were already sharing a version of this dream: the hope that the digital world would be a happy space of common understanding, free information, and collaboration. The internet was to be a "promised land" where people could rely on information shared on the basis of transparency, trust, and expertise.

PITFALLS TO AVOID

12. These expectations, however, were not exactly met.

First of all, we are still dealing with a "digital divide." While this evolution is moving faster than our capabilities to understand it properly, many people still lack access not only to basic needs, such as food, water, clothing, housing, and healthcare, but also to information-communication technologies. This leaves a great number of the marginalized stranded on the roadside.

Besides that, a "social media divide" is becoming ever more acute. Platforms that promise to build community and bring the world closer together have instead deepened various forms of division.

13. There are a few pitfalls to be aware of on the "digital highway," which allow us to understand better how this could happen.

Today it is not possible to talk about "social media" without considering its commercial value — that is, without the awareness that the actual revolution occurred when brands and institutions realized the strategic potential of social platforms, contributing to a rapid consolidation of languages and practices that over the years transformed *users* into *consumers*. Additionally, individuals are both *consumers* and *commodities*: As consumers, they are presented with *data-driven advertising* and sponsored content in a tailor-made way. As commodities, their profiles and data are sold to other businesses with the same end in mind. By adhering to the mission statements of social media companies, people also accept "terms of agreement" that they usually do not read or understand. It has become popular to understand these "terms of agreement" according to an old adage that says, "*If you are not paying for it, you are the product.*" In other words, it is not free: We are paying with minutes of our attention and bytes of our data.

14. Increasing emphasis on the distribution and trade of knowledge, data, and information has generated a paradox: In a society where information plays such an essential role, it is increasingly difficult to verify sources and the accuracy of the information that circulates digitally. Content overload is solved by artificial intelligence algorithms that

constantly determine what to show us based on factors that we hardly perceive or realize: not only our previous choices, likes, reactions or preferences, but also our absences and distractions, pauses, and attention spans. The digital environment that each person sees — and even the results of an online search — is never the same as that of someone else. By searching for information on browsers or receiving it in our feed for different platforms and applications, we are usually not aware of the filters that condition the results. The consequence of this increasingly sophisticated personalization of results is a forced exposure to partial information, which corroborates our own ideas, reinforces our beliefs, and thus leads us into an isolation of "*filter bubbles*."

15. Online communities on social media are "meeting points," usually shaped around the shared interests of "networked individuals." Those present on social media are addressed according to their particular characteristics, origins, tastes, and preferences, as the algorithms behind online platforms and search engines tend to bring those who are "sames" together, grouping them and drawing their attention in order to keep them online. Consequently, social media platforms can run the risk of preventing their users from really meeting the "other" who is different.

16. We have all witnessed automated systems that risk creating these individualistic "spaces," and at times encouraging extreme behaviors. Aggressive and negative speeches are easily and rapidly spread, offering a fertile field for violence, abuse, and misinformation. On social media, different actors, often emboldened by a cloak of pseudonymity, are con-

stantly reacting to each other. These interactions are usually markedly different from those in physical spaces, where our actions are influenced by verbal and nonverbal feedback from others.

17. Being aware of these pitfalls helps us to discern and unmask the logic that pollutes the social media environment and to search for a solution to such digital discontent. It is important to appreciate the digital world and recognize it as part of our life. It is, however, in the complementarity of digital and physical experiences that a human life and journey are built.

18. Along the "digital highways" many people are hurt by division and hatred. We cannot ignore it. We cannot be just silent passersby. In order to humanize digital environments, we must not forget those who are "left behind." We can only see what is going on if we look from the perspective of the wounded man in the parable of the good Samaritan. As in the parable, where we are informed about what the wounded man has seen, the perspective of the digitally marginalized and wounded helps us to understand better today's increasingly complex world.

WEAVING RELATIONSHIPS

19. In a time when we are increasingly divided, when each person retreats into his or her own filtered bubble, social media is becoming a path leading many toward indifference, polarization, and extremism. When individuals do not treat each other as human beings but as mere expressions of a certain point of view that they do not share, we witness another expression of the "throwaway culture"

that proliferates the "globalization" — and normalization — of indifference. Retreating into the isolation of one's own interests cannot be the way to restore hope. Rather, the way forward is the cultivation of a "culture of encounter," which promotes friendship and peace among different people.[9]

20. Therefore, there is an increasingly urgent need to engage social media platforms in a way that goes beyond one's silos, exiting the group of one's "sames" in order to meet others.

To welcome the "other," someone who takes positions opposed to my own or who seems "different," is certainly not an easy task. "Why should I care?" might well be our first reaction. We can even find this attitude in the Bible, starting with Cain's refusal to be his brother's keeper (cf. Gn 4:9) and continuing with the scribe who asked Jesus, "Who is my neighbor?" (Lk 10:29). The scribe wanted to set a limit regarding who *is* and who *is not* my neighbor. It seems that we would like to find a justification for our own indifference; we are always trying to draw a line between "us" and "them," between "someone I have to treat with respect" and "someone I can ignore." In this way, almost imperceptibly, we grow incapable of feeling compassion for others, as if their sufferings were their own responsibility and none of our business.[10]

21. The parable of the good Samaritan, instead, challenges us to confront the digital "throwaway culture" and help each other to step out of our comfort zone by making a voluntary effort to reach out to the other. This is only possible if we empty ourselves, understanding that each one of us is

part of wounded humanity, and remembering that someone has looked at us and had compassion on us.

22. It is only in this way that we can — and should — be the ones who make the first step in overcoming indifference, for we believe in a "God who is not indifferent."[11] We can and should be the ones who stop asking, "How much do I really have to care for others?" and begin instead to act as neighbors, rejecting the logic of exclusion and rebuilding a logic of community.[12] We can and should be the ones who move from the understanding of digital media as an individual experience to one that is founded upon mutual encounter, which fosters community building.

23. Instead of acting as individuals producing content or reacting to information, ideas and images shared by others, we need to ask: How can we cocreate healthier online experiences where people can engage in conversations and overcome disagreements with a spirit of mutual listening?

How can we empower communities to find ways to overcome divisions and promote dialogue and respect in social media platforms?

How can we restore the online environment to the place that it can and should be: a place of sharing, collaborating, and belonging, based on mutual trust?

24. Everyone can participate in bringing about this change by engaging with others, and by challenging themselves in their encounters with others. As believers, we are called to be communicators who move intentionally toward encoun-

ter. In this way, we can seek encounters that are meaningful and lasting, rather than superficial and ephemeral. Indeed, by orienting digital connections toward encountering real persons, forming real relationships, and building real community, we are actually nourishing our relationship with God. That said, our relationship with God must also be nourished through prayer and the sacramental life of the Church, which because of their essence can never be reduced simply to the "digital" realm.

II. FROM AWARENESS TO TRUE ENCOUNTER

Learning from the one who had compassion (cf. Lk 10:33).

INTENTIONAL LISTENERS

25. The reflection on our engagement with social media began with an awareness of how these networks work and the opportunities and challenges we face in them. If online social networks bear an inherent temptation toward individualism and self-aggrandizement, as described in the preceding chapter, we are not condemned willy-nilly to fall into these attitudes. The disciple who has encountered the merciful gaze of Christ has experienced something else. He or she knows that communicating well begins with listening and an awareness that another person is before me. Listening and awareness aim to foster encounter and to overcome existing obstacles, including the obstacle of indifference. Listening in this manner is an essential step in engaging others; it is a first indispensable ingredient for communication and a condition for genuine dialogue.[13]

26. In the parable of the good Samaritan, the man who was beaten and left to die was helped by the least expected person: In Jesus' time, the Jewish and Samaritan peoples were often at odds. If anything, hostility would have been the expected behavior. The Samaritan, however, did not see that beaten man as an "other," but simply as someone who need-

ed help. He felt compassion, putting himself in the other's shoes, and gave of himself, his time, and his resources to listen to and accompany someone he encountered.[14]

27. This parable can inspire social media relationships because it illustrates the possibility of a profoundly meaningful encounter between two complete strangers. The Samaritan breaks down the "social divide": He reaches beyond the boundaries of agreement and disagreement. While the priest and Levite pass by the wounded man, the Samaritan traveler sees him and has compassion (cf. Lk 10:33). Compassion means feeling that the other person is a part of myself. The Samaritan listens to the man's story; he draws near because he is moved from within.

28. The Gospel of Luke does not include any dialogue between the two men. We can imagine the Samaritan finding the wounded man and, perhaps, asking him, "What happened to you?" But even without words, through his attitude of openness and hospitality, an encounter begins. That first gesture is an expression of care, and this is crucial. The ability to listen and be open to receiving the story of another without concern for the cultural prejudices of the time prevented the wounded man from being left for dead.

29. The interaction between the two men prompts us to make the first move in the digital world. We are invited to see the value and dignity of those with whom we have differences. We are also invited to look beyond our safety net, our silos, and our bubbles. Becoming a neighbor in the social media environment requires intentionality. And it all begins with the ability to listen well, to let the reality of the other touch us.

ROBBING OUR ATTENTION

30. Listening is a fundamental skill that allows us to enter relationships with others and not just engage in the exchange of information. Our devices, however, are replete with information. We find ourselves embedded in an information network, connecting with others through shared postings of text, images, and sound. Social media platforms allow us to scroll endlessly as we explore this context. While video and sound have certainly increased the media richness of digital communication, our mediated interactions with one another still remain limited. We often encounter information quickly and without the full and necessary context. We can react easily and rapidly to information on a screen without seeking the full story.

31. This abundance of information has many benefits: When we are part of the network, information is promptly and widely accessible and personalized to our interests. We can gain practical information, maintain social connections, explore resources, and deepen and expand our knowledge. The ease of access to information and communication also has the potential to create inclusive spaces that give voice to those in our communities who are marginalized by social or economic injustice.

32. At the same time, the endless availability of information has also created some challenges. We experience *information overload* as our cognitive ability to process suffers from the excessive information available to us. In a similar vein, we experience *social interaction overload* as we are subject to a high level of social solicitations. Different websites, applications, and platforms are programmed to prey on our

human desire for acknowledgment, and they are constantly fighting for people's attention. Attention itself has become the most valuable asset and commodity.

33. In this environment, our attention is not focused, as we attempt to navigate this overwhelming information and social interaction network. Instead of focusing on one issue at a time, our *continuous partial attention* rapidly passes from one topic to the other. In our "always on" condition, we face the temptation to post instantly since we are physiologically hooked on digital stimulation, always wanting more content in endless scrolling, and [become] frustrated by any lack of updates. One significant cognitive challenge of digital culture is the loss of our ability to think deeply and purposefully. We scan the surface and remain in the shallows instead of deeply pondering realities.

34. We must be more mindful in this regard. Without silence and the space to think slowly, deeply, and purposefully, we risk losing not only cognitive capacities, but also the depth of our interactions, both human and divine. The space for deliberate listening, attentiveness, and discernment of the truth is becoming rare.

The process called *attention-interest-desire-action*, well-known to advertisers, is similar to the process through which any temptation enters into the human heart and draws our attention away from the only word that is really meaningful and life-giving, the Word of God. In one way or another, we are still paying attention to the old serpent who shows us new fruits every day. They seem "good for food and pleasing to the eye, and also desirable for gaining wisdom" (Gn 3:6). Like seeds along the path, where the word is sown, we allow the evil one to come and take away the word that was sown in us (cf. Mk 4:14–15).

35. With this overload of stimuli and data that we receive, silence is a precious commodity, for it ensures space for focus and discernment.[15] The impetus to seek silence in digital culture elevates the importance of focusing and listening. In educational or work environments, as well as in families and communities, there is a growing need to detach ourselves from digital devices. "Silence" in this case can be compared to a "digital detox," which is not simply a withdrawal, but rather a way to engage more deeply with God and with others.

36. Listening emerges from silence and is fundamental for caring for others. By listening we welcome someone, we offer hospitality and show that person respect. To listen is also an act of humility on our part, as we acknowledge truth, wisdom, and value beyond our own limited perspective. Without a listening disposition, we are not able to receive the gift of another.

WITH THE EAR OF THE HEART

37. With the speed and immediacy of the digital culture, which tests our attentiveness and ability to focus, listening becomes all the more important in our spiritual lives. A contemplative approach is countercultural, prophetic even, and may be formative not only for persons but for culture as a whole.

A commitment to listening on social media is a fundamental starting point for moving toward a network that is not so much about bytes, avatars, and "likes," but of people.[16] In this way we move from rapid reactions, misleading assumptions, and impulsive comments to creating opportunities for dialogue, raising questions to learn more, demonstrating care and compassion, and recognizing the dignity of those we encounter.

38. Digital culture has immeasurably increased our access to others. This also affords us the opportunity to listen to much more. Often when speaking of "listening" in social media, reference is made to data-monitoring processes, engagement statistics, and actions aimed at a marketing analysis of the social behaviors present on the networks. This, of course, is not enough for social media to be an environment for listening and dialogue. Intentional listening in the digital context calls for listening with the "ear of the heart." To listen with the ear of the heart goes beyond the physical ability to hear sounds. Instead, it impels us to be open to the other with the whole of our being: *an openness of the heart that makes closeness possible.*[17] It is a posture of attentiveness and hospitality that is fundamental for establishing communication. This wisdom applies not only to contemplative prayer, but also to people seeking authentic relationships and genuine communities. The desire to be in relationship with others and with the Other — God — remains a fundamental human need, one that is also evident in the desire for connectedness in digital culture.[18]

39. An inner dialogue and a relationship with God, made possible by the divine gift of faith, are essential in allowing us to grow in our ability to listen well. The Word of God

also has a fundamental role in this inner dialogue. Prayerful listening to the Word in Scripture through the practice of spiritual reading of biblical texts, such as *lectio divina,* can be profoundly formative as it allows for a slow, deliberate, and contemplative experience.[19]

40. The "Word of the Day" or "Gospel of the Day" are among the topics most googled by Christians, and it is safe to say that the digital environment has offered us many new and easier possibilities for a regular "meeting" with the divine Word. Our encounter with the Word of the living God, even online, shifts our approach from seeing information on the screen to encountering another person telling a story. If we keep in mind that we are connecting with other people behind the screen, the exercise of listening can extend hospitality to the stories of others and begin forging relationships.

DISCERNING OUR SOCIAL MEDIA PRESENCE

41. From the perspective of faith, what to communicate and how to communicate is not only a practical question, but also a spiritual one. Being present on social media platforms prompts discernment. Communicating well in these contexts is an exercise in prudence and calls for prayerful consideration of how to engage with others. Approaching this question through the lens of the scribe's question, "Who is my neighbor?", calls for discernment regarding God's presence in and through the way we relate with one another on social media platforms.

42. On social media, neighborliness is a complex concept. Social media "neighbors" are most clearly those with whom we maintain connections. At the same time, our neighbors

are also often those we cannot see, either because platforms prevent us from seeing them or because they are simply not there. Digital environments are also shared by other participants such as "internet bots" and "deepfakes," automated computer programs that operate online with assigned tasks, often simulating human action or collecting data.

Additionally, social media platforms are controlled by an external "authority," usually a for-profit organization that develops, manages, and promotes changes to how the platform is programmed to work. In a broader sense, these all "live in" or contribute to the online "neighborhood."

43. Recognizing our digital neighbor is about recognizing that every person's life concerns us, even when his or her presence (or absence) is mediated by digital means. "Today's media do enable us to communicate and to share our knowledge and affections," as Pope Francis says in *Laudato Si'*, "yet at times they also shield us from direct contact with the pain, the fears, and the joys of others and the complexity of their personal experiences."[20] To be neighborly on social media means being present to the stories of others, especially those who are suffering. In other words, advocating for better digital environments does not mean taking the focus off the concrete problems experienced by many people — for example, hunger, poverty, forced migration, war, disease, and loneliness. It means, instead, advocating for an integral vision of human life that, today, includes the digital realm. In fact, social media can be one way to draw more attention to these realities and build solidarity among those near and far.

44. In viewing social media as a space not only for connections but ultimately for relationships, a proper "examination of conscience" regarding our presence on social media should include three vital relationships: with God, our neighbor, and the environment around us.[21] Our relationships with others and our environment should nourish our relationship with God, and our relationship with God, which is the most important, must be visible in our relationships with others and with our environment.

III. FROM ENCOUNTER TO COMMUNITY

"Look after him" (cf. Lk 10:35) — extending the healing process to others.

FACE TO FACE

45. Communication begins with connection and moves toward relationships, community, and communion.[22] There is no communication without the truth of an encounter. To communicate is to establish relationships; it is to "be with." To be community is to share with others fundamental truths about what one holds and what one is. Far beyond mere geographic-territorial or ethnic-cultural proximity, what constitutes a community is a common sharing of truth together with a sense of belonging, reciprocity, and solidarity in the different spheres of social life. When considering these latter elements, it is important to remember that the construction of communal unity through communicative practices, which maintain social ties across time and space, will be always secondary with respect to the adherence to truth itself.

46. How to build a community through communicative practices even among those who are not physically near to each other is actually a very old question. We can identify a tension between mediated presence and a longing for in-person meeting already in the letters of the apostles. The evangelist John, for example, concludes his second and

third letter by saying: "I have much to write to you, but I do not want to use paper and ink. Instead, I hope to visit you and talk with you face to face, so that our joy may be complete" (2 Jn 12). The same is true for the apostle Paul, who, even in his absence and his "longing to see" the people in person (cf. 1 Thes 2:17), was present through his letters in the life of every community he founded (1 Cor 5:3). His writings also served to "interconnect" the different communities (Col 4:15–16). Paul's community-building capacity has been transmitted to our day through his many letters, where we learn that for him there was no dichotomy between physical presence and presence through his written word read by the community (2 Cor 10:9–11).

47. In the increasingly *onlife* reality of today's world, it is necessary to overcome an either-or logic, which thinks of human relationships within a dichotomous logic (*digital* vs. *real/physical/in person*), and assume a "both-and" logic, based on the complementarity and wholeness of human and social life. Community relations on social media networks should strengthen local communities and vice versa. "The use of the *social web* is complementary to an encounter in the flesh that comes alive through the body, heart, eyes, gaze, and breath of the other. If the net is used as an extension or expectation of such an encounter, then the network concept is not betrayed and remains a resource for communion."[23] "The digital world can be an environment rich in humanity; a network not of wires but of people,"[24] if we remember that on the other side of the screen there are no "numbers" or mere "aggregates of individuals," but people who have stories, dreams, expectations, sufferings. There is a name and a face.

ON THE ROAD TO JERICHO

48. Digital media allows people to meet beyond the boundaries of space and cultures. Even though these digital encounters may not necessarily bring physical closeness, they can be nonetheless meaningful, impactful, and real. Beyond mere connections, they can be an avenue to engage sincerely with others, to engage in meaningful conversations, to express solidarity, and to relieve someone's isolation and pain.

49. Social media can be seen as another "road to Jericho," replete with opportunities for unplanned encounters as it was for Jesus: a blind beggar shouting loudly at the roadside (cf. Lk 18:35–43), a dishonest tax collector hiding in the branches of a sycamore tree (Lk 19:1–9), a wounded man left half dead by the robbers (Lk 10:30). At the same time, the parable of the good Samaritan reminds us that just because someone is "religious" (a priest or Levite) or claims to be a follower of Jesus, it is not a guarantee that they will offer help or seek healing and reconciliation. The blind man was rebuked by Jesus' disciples and told to be quiet; Zacchaeus' interaction with Jesus was accompanied by other people's grumbling; the wounded man was simply ignored by the priest and the Levite as they passed by.

50. In the digital crossroads, as in face-to-face encounters, being "Christian" is not enough. It is possible to find many profiles or accounts on social media that proclaim religious content but do not engage in relational dynamics in a faithful way. Hostile interactions and violent, degrading words, especially in the context of sharing Christian content, cry out from the screen and are a contradiction to the Gospel itself.[25]

On the contrary, the good Samaritan, who is attentive and open to encountering the wounded man, is moved with compassion to act and to care for him. He tends to the victim's wounds and takes him to an inn to ensure his ongoing care. Likewise, our desires to make social media a more human and relational space must be translated into concrete attitudes and creative gestures.

51. Fostering a sense of community includes being attentive to shared values, experiences, hopes, sorrows, joys, humor, and even jokes, that in and of themselves can become gathering points for people in digital spaces. As with listening, discernment, and encountering, forming community with others requires personal commitment. What is defined as "friendship" by social media platforms begins simply as a connection or familiarity. However, there, too, it is possible to emphasize a shared spirit of support and companionship. To become community requires a free and mutual sense of participation; to become a desired association that gathers members based on proximity. Freedom and mutual support do not emerge automatically. In order to form community, the work of healing and reconciliation is often the first step to be taken along the way.

52. Even on social media, "we have to decide whether to be good Samaritans or indifferent bystanders. And if we extend our gaze to the history of our own lives and that of the entire world, all of us are, or have been, like each of the characters in the parable. All of us have in ourselves something of the wounded man, something of the robber, something of the passersby, and something of the good Samaritan."[26]

All of us can be passersby on the digital highways — simply "connected"[27] — or we can do something like the Samaritan and allow connections to grow into true encounters. The casual passerby becomes a neighbor when he cares for the wounded man by dressing his wounds. In caring for the man, he aims to heal not only the physical wounds, but also the divisions and animosity that exist between their social groups.

53. What does it mean, then, to "heal" the wounds on social media? How can we "bind up" division? How can we build ecclesial environments capable of welcoming and integrating the "geographical and existential peripheries" of today's cultures? Questions like these are essential for discerning our Christian presence on the digital highways.

"Today we have a great opportunity to express our innate sense of fraternity, to be good Samaritans who bear the pain of other people's troubles rather than fomenting greater hatred and resentment. Like the chance traveler in the parable, we need only have a pure and simple desire to be a people, a community, constant and tireless in the effort to include, integrate, and lift up the fallen."[28]

"GO AND DO LIKEWISE"

54. Relationship begets relationship, community builds community. The grace of the relationship that is established between two people moves beyond their interaction. The human person is made for relationship and community. At the same time, loneliness and isolation plague our cultural reality, as we acutely experienced during the COVID-19 pandemic. Those seeking company, especially the margin-

alized, often turn to digital spaces to find community, inclusion, and solidarity with others. While many have found solace in connecting with others in digital space, others find it inadequate. We may be failing to provide space for those seeking to engage in dialogue and find support without experiencing judgmental or defensive attitudes.

55. The movement from encounter to relationship and then community speaks to both the gifts and challenges of digital culture. Sometimes online communities form when people find common ground in gathering points against an external "other," a common ideological enemy. This kind of polarization yields a "digital tribalism" wherein groups are pitted against others in an adversarial spirit. We cannot forget the presence of others, brothers and sisters, persons of dignity across these tribal lines. We "must not categorize others in order to decide who is my neighbor and who is not. It is up to me whether to be a neighbor or not — the decision is mine — it is up to me whether or not to be a neighbor to those whom I encounter, who need help, even if they are strangers or perhaps hostile."[29] Unfortunately, broken relationships, conflicts, and divisions are not foreign to the Church. For example, when groups that present themselves as "Catholic" use their social media presence to foster division, they are not behaving like a Christian community should.[30] Instead of capitalizing on conflicts and adversarial clickbait, hostile attitudes should become opportunities for conversion, an opportunity to witness encounter, dialogue, and reconciliation around seemingly divisive matters.[31]

56. Engagement with social media must go beyond the exchange of personal opinions or the emulation of behaviors.

Social action mobilized through social media has had a greater impact and is often more effective in transforming the world than a superficial debate regarding ideas. The debates are usually limited by the number of characters allowed and the speed with which people react to comments, not to mention emotional ad hominem arguments — attacks directed at the person speaking regardless of the overall topic being discussed.

Sharing ideas is necessary, but ideas alone do not work; they must become "flesh." Actions must fertilize the ground day after day.[32]

Learning from the Samaritan, we are called to become attentive to this dynamic. He does not stop at feeling pity; he does not even stop at bandaging a stranger's wounds. He goes further, taking the injured man to an inn and arranging for his continued care.[33] Through this arrangement, the relationship of care and the seeds of community established between the Samaritan and the wounded man are extended to the innkeeper and his household.

Like the scholar of the law, we, too, in our digital media presence, are invited to "go and do likewise" and so promote the common good. How can we help heal a toxic digital environment? How can we promote hospitality and opportunities for healing and reconciliation?

57. Hospitality builds on the openness we bring to encountering the other; through it, we welcome Christ in the guise of the stranger (cf. Mt 25:40). For this, digital communities must share content and interests, but also act together

and become a witness for communion. There are already powerful expressions of communities of care in the digital context. For example, there are communities that gather to support others in times of illness, loss, and grief, as well as communities that crowdfund for someone in need and those who provide social and psychological support among members. All these efforts can be considered examples of "digital proximity." People who are very different from each other can engage in an online "dialogue of social action." They may or may not be inspired by faith. In any case, communities that are formed to act for the good of others are key to overcoming isolation in social media.

58. We can think even bigger: The social web is not cast in stone. We can change it. We can become drivers of change, imagining new models built on trust, transparency, equality, and inclusion. Together, we can urge media companies to reconsider their roles and let the internet become a truly public space. Well-structured public spaces are able to promote better social behavior. We need, therefore, to rebuild digital spaces so that they will become more human and healthier environments.

SHARING A MEAL

59. As a community of faith, the Church is on pilgrimage toward the kingdom of heaven. Since social media and, more broadly, digital reality is a crucial aspect of this journey, it is important to reflect on the dynamics of communion and community vis-à-vis the Church's presence in the digital environment.

During the most severe moments of lockdown during the

pandemic, the broadcasting of liturgical celebrations via social media and other means of communication offered some comfort to those who could not participate in person. However, there is still much to reflect on in our faith communities about how to take advantage of the digital environment in a way that complements sacramental life. Theological and pastoral questions have been raised regarding various topics — for example, commercial exploitation of the retransmission of holy Mass.

60. The ecclesial community is formed where two or three gather in the name of Jesus (cf. Mt 18:20) regardless of one's origin, residence, or geographical affiliation. While we can recognize that through the transmission of the Mass the Church has entered into people's homes, it is necessary to reflect on what "participation" in the Eucharist means.[34] The emergence of the digital culture and the experience of the pandemic have revealed how much our pastoral initiatives have paid little attention to the "domestic Church," the Church that gathers in homes and around the table. In this regard, we need to rediscover the link between the liturgy that is celebrated in our churches and the celebration of the Lord with the gestures, words, and prayers in the family home. Put another way, we need to rebuild the bridge between our family tables and the altar, where we are spiritually nourished through our reception of the holy Eucharist and confirmed in our communion as believers.

61. One cannot share a meal through a screen.[35] All our senses are engaged when we share a meal: taste and smell, glances that contemplate the faces of the diners, listening to the conversations at table. Sharing a meal at table is our first

education in attention to others, a fostering of relationships among family members, neighbors, friends, and colleagues. Likewise, we participate with the whole person at the altar: mind, spirit, and body are involved. The liturgy is a sensory experience; we enter into the Eucharistic mystery through the doors of the senses that are awakened and fed in their need for beauty, meaning, harmony, vision, interaction, and emotion. Above all, the Eucharist is not something that we can just "watch"; it is something that truly nourishes us.

62. Embodiment is important for Christians. The Word of God became incarnate in a body, he suffered and died with his body, and he rose again in the resurrection in his body. After he returned to the Father, everything that he went through in his body flowed into the sacraments.[36] He entered into the heavenly sanctuary and left open a pilgrim way through which heaven is poured out upon us.

63. Being connected beyond the boundaries of space is not an achievement of "wonderful technological discoveries." It is something we experience, even without knowing it, each time we "gather in the name of Jesus," each time we participate in the universal communion of the body of Christ. There, we connect with the heavenly Jerusalem and meet the saints of all times and acknowledge each other as parts of the same Body of Christ.

Therefore, as Pope Francis reminds us in his 2019 World Communications Day Message, the *social web* complements — but does not substitute for — an encounter in the flesh that comes alive through the body, heart, eyes, gaze, and breath of the other. "If a family uses the net to be more connected, to then meet at table and look into each other's eyes, then it is a resource. If a Church community coordinates its activity through the network and then celebrates the Eucharist together, then it is a resource. ... The Church herself is a network woven together by Eucharistic communion, where unity is based not on 'likes,' but on the truth, on the 'Amen,' by which each one clings to the Body of Christ, and welcomes others."[37]

IV. A DISTINCTIVE STYLE

Love ... and you will live (cf. Lk 10:27–28).

THE *WHAT* AND THE *HOW*: THE CREATIVITY OF LOVE

64. Many Christian content creators ask themselves: What is the most effective strategy to reach more users/persons/souls? What tool makes my content more attractive? What style works best? While these questions are helpful, we should always remember that communication is not simply a "strategy." It is much more. A true communicator gives everything, gives all of himself or herself. We communicate with our soul and with our body, with our mind, our heart, our hands, with everything.[38]

By sharing the Bread of Life, we learn a "style of sharing" from the One who loved us and gave himself for us (cf. Gal 2:20). This style is reflected in three attitudes — "closeness, compassion and tenderness" — that Pope Francis recognizes as distinctive characteristics of God's style.[39] Jesus himself, in his farewell dinner, assured us that the distinctive sign of his disciples would be to love one another as he has loved them. By this, everyone is able to recognize a Christian community (Jn 13:34–35).

HOW MIGHT ONE REFLECT GOD'S "STYLE" ON SOCIAL MEDIA?

65. First of all, we should remember that whatever we share in our posts, comments, and likes, in spoken or written

words, in film or animated images, should align with the style that we learn from Christ, who transmitted his message not only in speech but in the whole manner of his life, revealing that communication, at its most profound level, is the giving of self in love.[40] Therefore, *how* we say something is just as important as *what* we say. All creativity lies in ensuring that the *how* corresponds to the *what*. In other words, we can only communicate well if we "love well."[41]

66. To communicate truth, we must first make sure that we are conveying truthful information — not only in creating content, but also in sharing it. We must make sure that we are a trusted source. To communicate goodness, we need quality content, a message that is oriented to help, not to harm; to promote positive action, not to waste time in useless discussions. To communicate beauty, we need to make sure that we are communicating a message in its entirety, which needs the art of contemplation — an art that enables us to see a reality or an event linked to many other realities and events.

In the context of "post-truth" and "fake news," Jesus Christ, "the way and the truth and the life" (Jn 14:6), represents the principle for our communion with God and one another.[42] As Pope Francis reminded us in the 2019 World Communication Day message: "The duty to guard the truth springs from the need not to belie the mutual relationship of communion. Truth is revealed in communion. Lies, on the other hand, are a selfish refusal to recognize that we are members of one body; they are a refusal to give ourselves to others, thus losing the only way to find ourselves."[43]

67. For this reason, the second thing to remember is that a message is more easily persuasive when the one who communicates it belongs to a community. There is an urgent need to act not merely as individuals, but as communities. The fact that social media facilitates individual initiatives in content production could seem like a valuable opportunity, but it can become problematic when individual activities are carried out capriciously and do not reflect the overall goal and outlook of the Church community. Setting aside our own agenda and the affirmation of our own abilities and skills, in order to discover that each one of us — with all our talents and weaknesses — is part of a group, is a gift that empowers us to collaborate as "members of one another." We are called to give witness to a style of communication that fosters our belonging to one another, and that revives what Saint Paul calls the "joints" that enable the members of a body to act in synergy (Col 2:19).

68. Our creativity can thus only be an outcome of communion: It is not so much the achievement of a great individual genius, but rather the fruit of a great friendship. In other words, it is the fruit of love. As Christian communicators we are called to bear witness to a style of communication that is not just based on the individual, but on a way of community building and belonging. The best way to convey content is to put together the voices of those who love that content. Working together as a team, making space for diverse talents, backgrounds, capacities, and rhythms, co-creating beauty in a "symphonic creativity," is actually the most beautiful witness that we are really children of God, redeemed from being concerned only with ourselves and open to an encounter with others.

TELL IT WITH A STORY

69. Good stories capture the attention and engage the imagination. They reveal and extend hospitality to the truth. Stories give us an interpretive framework to understand the world and to answer our deepest questions. Stories build community, for community is always built through communication.

Storytelling has acquired a renewed importance in digital culture because of the unique power of stories to grab our attention and speak to us directly; they also provide a fuller context for communication than is possible in truncated posts or tweets. Digital culture is replete with information, and its platforms are mostly chaotic environments. Stories offer a structure, a way to make sense of the digital experience. More "enfleshed" than a mere argument and more complex than the superficial and emotional reactions often encountered on digital platforms, they help to restore human relationships by offering people the opportunity to convey their stories or share those that have transformed them.

70. A good reason to tell a story is to respond to people who question our message or our mission. Creating a counter-narrative can be more effective in replying to a hateful comment than answering with an argument.[44] In this way we shift the attention from defense to the active promotion of a positive message and the cultivation of solidarity, as Jesus did with the story of the good Samaritan. Instead of arguing with the expert in the law about whom we should consider our neighbor and whom we can ignore or even hate, Jesus simply told a story. As a master storyteller, Jesus does not put

the lawyer in the shoes of the Samaritan, but in the shoes of the wounded man. To find out who his neighbor is, he must first understand that he is in the shoes of the wounded man and that another has had compassion on him. Only when the lawyer has discovered this, and has experienced the Samaritan's care for him, can he draw conclusions about his own life and make the story his own. The lawyer himself is the man who has fallen into the hands of the robbers, and the Samaritan approaching him is Jesus.

Each one of us, listening to this story, is the wounded man lying there. And for each one of us, the Samaritan is Jesus. For if we still ask, "Who is my neighbor?", it is because we still have not experienced that we are loved and that our life is connected to every life.

71. From the beginnings of the Church, telling the story of the profound experience that Jesus' followers had in his presence attracted others to Christian discipleship. The Acts of the Apostles are full of such examples. For instance, Peter was empowered by the Holy Spirit and preached the resurrection of Christ to the pilgrims on Pentecost. This led to the conversion of three thousand people (cf. Acts 2:14-41). Here we get an idea of how much our storytelling can influence others. At the same time, recounting stories and experiences is just one element of evangelization. Systematic explanations of the Faith done through the formulation of creeds and other doctrinal works are also important.

BUILDING COMMUNITY IN A FRAGMENTED WORLD

72. People search for somebody that can give direction and

hope; they are hungry for moral and spiritual leadership, but they do not often find it in traditional places. It is common now to turn to "influencers," individuals who gain and maintain a large following, who acquire greater visibility and are able to inspire and motivate others with their ideas or experiences. Adopted from public-opinion theory for the social media marketing approach, the success of a social media influencer is linked to his or her ability to stand out in the vastness of the network by attracting a large number of followers.

73. In itself, going "viral" is a neutral action; it does not automatically have a positive or a negative impact on the lives of others. In this regard: "Social networks can facilitate relationships and promote the good of society, but they can also lead to further polarization and division between individuals and groups. The digital world is a public square, a meeting place where we can either encourage or demean one another, engage in a meaningful discussion or unfair attacks."[45]

74. *Micro- and macro-influencers*
We should all take our "influence" seriously. There are not only macro-influencers with a large audience, but also micro-influencers. Every Christian is a micro-influencer. Every Christian should be aware of his or her potential influence, no matter how many followers he or she has. At the same time, he or she needs to be aware that the value of the message conveyed by the Christian "influencer" does not depend on the qualities of the messenger. Every follower of Christ has the potential to establish a link, not to himself or herself, but to the kingdom of God, even for the smallest cir-

cle of his or her relationships. "Believe in the Lord Jesus, and you will be saved — you and your household" (Acts 16:31).

However, we should recognize that our responsibility increases with the increase in the number of followers. The greater the number of followers, the greater our awareness should be that we are not acting in our own name. The responsibility to minister to one's community, especially for those in public leadership roles, cannot become secondary to promoting one's personal opinions from the public pulpits of digital media.[46]

75. *Be reflective, not reactive*
The Christian style should be reflective, not reactive, on social media. Therefore, we should all be careful not to fall into the digital traps hidden in content that is intentionally designed to sow conflict among users by causing outrage or emotional reactions.

We must be mindful of posting and sharing content that can cause misunderstanding, exacerbate division, incite conflict, and deepen prejudices. Unfortunately, the tendency to get carried away in heated and sometimes disrespectful discussions is common with online exchanges. We can all fall into the temptation of looking for the "speck in the eye" of our brothers and sisters (cf. Mt 7:3) by making public accusations on social media, stirring up divisions within the Church community or arguing about who among us is the greatest, as the first disciples did (Lk 9:46). The problem of polemical and superficial, and thus divisive, communication is particularly worrying when it comes from Church leadership: bishops, pastors, and prominent lay leaders.

These not only cause division in the community, but also give permission and legitimacy for others likewise to promote similar types of communication.

In the face of this temptation, often the best course of action is not to react, or to react with silence so as not to dignify this false dynamic. It is safe to say that this kind of dynamic does not build up; on the contrary, it causes great harm. Thus Christians are called to show another way.

76. *Be active, be synodal*
Social media can become an opportunity to share stories and experiences of beauty or suffering that are physically distant from us. In doing so, then, we can pray together and seek out the good together, rediscovering what unites us.[47] Being active means engaging in projects that affect people's everyday lives: projects that promote human dignity and development, aim to reduce digital inequality, promote digital access to information and literacy, promote stewardship and crowdfunding initiatives in favor of those who are poor and marginalized, and give voice to the voiceless in society.

The challenges that we face are global and thus require a global collaborative effort. It is urgent then to learn to act together, as a community and not as individuals. Not so much as individual influencers, but as "weavers of communion": pooling our talents and skills, sharing knowledge and contributions.[48]

For this reason, Jesus sent out the disciples "two by two" (Mk 6:7), so that by walking together[49] we can reveal, also on social media, the synodal face of the Church. This is the profound meaning of the communion that unites all the baptized all over the world. As Christians, communion is part of our "DNA." As such, the Holy Spirit enables us to open our hearts to others and embrace our membership in a universal fraternity.

THE MARK OF WITNESS

77. Our social media presence usually focuses on spreading information. Along these lines, presenting ideas, teachings, thoughts, spiritual reflections, and the like on social media needs to be faithful to the Christian tradition. But that is not enough. In addition to our ability to reach others with interesting religious content, we Christians should be known for our availability to listen, to discern before acting, to treat all people with respect, to respond with a question rather than a judgment, to remain silent rather than trigger a controversy, and to be "quick to hear, slow to speak, slow to anger" (Jas 1:19). In other words, all that we do, in word and deed, should bear the mark of witness. We are not present in social media to "sell a product." We are not advertising but communicating life, the life that was given to us in Christ. Therefore, every Christian must be careful not to proselytize, but give witness.

78. What does it mean to be a witness? The Greek word for witness is "martyr," and it is safe to say that some of the most powerful "Christian influencers" have been martyrs. The attractiveness of the martyrs is that they manifest their union with God through the sacrifice of their very lives.[50] "Do you not know that your bodies are temples of the Holy Spirit, who is in you, whom you have received from God? You are

not your own" (1 Cor 6:19). The bodies of martyrs are exemplary instruments for the revelation of the love of God.

While martyrdom is the ultimate sign of Christian witness, every Christian is called to sacrifice himself or herself: Christian living is a vocation that consumes our very existence by offering ourselves, soul and body, to become a space for the communication of God's love, a sign pointing toward the Son of God.

It is in this sense that we better understand the words of the great John the Baptist, the first witness of Christ: "He must increase; I must decrease" (Jn 3:30). Like the forerunner, who urged his disciples to follow Christ, we too are not pursuing "followers" for ourselves, but for Christ. We can spread the Gospel only by forging a communion that unites us in Christ. We do this by following Jesus' example of interacting with others.

79. The attractiveness of faith reaches people where they are and how they are in the here and now. From being an unknown carpenter from Nazareth, Jesus quickly gained popularity all around the region of Galilee. Looking with compassion at the people, who were like sheep without a shepherd, Jesus proclaimed the kingdom of God by healing the sick and teaching the crowds. To assure the maximum "reach," he would often speak to the multitudes from a mountain or from a boat. To promote the "engagement" of some of his number, he chose twelve, and to them he explained everything. But then, unexpectedly, at the height of his "success," he would retreat into solitude with the Father. And he would ask his disciples to do the same: When

they were recounting the success of their missions, he invited them to come away to rest and pray. And when they were discussing who among them was the greatest, he announced to them his future suffering on the cross. His objective — they would understand it only later — was not to increase his audience, but to reveal the love of the Father so that people, all people, may have life and have it to the full (cf. Jn 10:10).

Following in the footsteps of Jesus, we should make it a priority to allot enough space for personal conversation with the Father and to remain in tune with the Holy Spirit, who will always remind us that everything has been reversed on the cross. There were no "likes" and almost no "followers" at the moment of the biggest manifestation of the glory of God! Every human measurement of success is relativized by the logic of the Gospel.

80. This is our witness: to vouch, with our words and our lives, for what someone else has done.[51] In this sense, and only in this sense, can we be witnesses — missionaries even — of Christ and his Spirit. This includes our engagement with social media. Faith means above all bearing witness to the joy that the Lord gives to us. And this joy always shines brightly against the backdrop of a grateful memory. Telling others about the reason for our hope and doing it with gentleness and respect (cf. 1 Pt 3:15) is a sign of gratitude. It is the response of one who, through gratitude, is made docile to the Spirit and is therefore free. This was true for Mary, who without wanting or trying, became *the most influential woman in history*.[52] It is the response of one who by the grace of humility does not put himself or herself in the

foreground and thus facilitates the encounter with Christ who said: "Learn from me, for I am meek and humble of heart" (Mt 11:29).

Following the logic of the Gospel, all we have to do is to provoke a question to awaken the search. The rest is the hidden work of God.

• • •

81. As we have seen, we travel the digital highways alongside friends and complete strangers, striving to avoid many pitfalls along the way, and we find ourselves becoming aware of the wounded on the side of the road. At times, these wounded may be other people. Sometimes we are the wounded ones. When this happens, we pause, and through the life we have received in the sacraments, which is at work in us, this awareness becomes encounter: from characters or images on a screen, the wounded man takes on the contours of a neighbor, a brother or sister, and indeed, the Lord, who said, "Whatever you do to one of the least of these ... you did it to me" (Mt 25:40). And if at times we are also the ones who are wounded, the Samaritan bending over us with compassion also bears the face of the Lord, who became our neighbor, bending over suffering humanity to tend to our wounds.

In either case, what might have begun as a chance meeting or distracted presence on social media platforms becomes people present to one another in an encounter filled with mercy. This mercy allows us to taste, already now, the kingdom of God, and the communion that has its origin in the

Holy Trinity: the true "promised land."

82. It may be, then, that from our loving, genuine presence in these digital spheres of human life, a pathway can be opened to that which Saint John and Saint Paul longed for in their letters: the face-to-face encounter of every wounded person with the Lord's Body, the Church, so that in a personal, heart-to-heart encounter, their wounds and ours may be healed, and "our joy may be complete" (2 Jn 12).

• • •

May the image of the good Samaritan, who tended to the wounds of the injured man by pouring oil and wine over them, be our inspiration. Let our communication be a balm that relieves pain and a fine wine that gladdens hearts. May the light we bring to others not be the result of cosmetics or special effects, but rather of our being loving and merciful "neighbors" to those wounded and left on the side of the road.[53]

Vatican City, May 28, 2023, Solemnity of Pentecost

Paolo Ruffini
Prefect

Lucio A. Ruiz
Secretary

NOTES

1. Synod of Bishops, *Final Document from the Pre-Synodal Meeting in Preparation for the XV Ordinary General Assembly*, "Young People, Faith and Vocational Discernment," Rome (March 19–24, 2018), 4.

2. *Message of His Holiness Pope Benedict XVI for the 43rd World Communications Day*, "New Technologies, New Relationships. Promoting a Culture of Respect, Dialogue and Friendship" (May 24, 2009). *Aetatis Novae* refers to digital technology already in 1992, and the 2002 companion documents *Ethics in Internet* and *Church in Internet* focus on the cultural impact of the internet in greater detail. Finally, St. John Paul II's 2005 apostolic letter *The Rapid Development*, addressed to those responsible for communication, offers reflections on questions raised by social communication. In addition to documents that specifically concern social communication, in recent decades other magisterial documents have also devoted sections to this theme. See for example *Verbum Domini*, 113; *Evangelii Gaudium*, 62, 70, 87; *Laudato Si'*, 47, 102–114; *Gaudete et Exsultate*, 115; *Christus Vivit*, 86–90, 104–106; *Fratelli Tutti*, 42–50).

3. *Message of His Holiness Pope Benedict XVI for the 47th World Communications Day*, "Social Networks, Portals of Truth and Faith, New Spaces for Evangelization" (January 24, 2013).

4. *Message of His Holiness Pope Francis for the 53rd World Communications Day*, "We are members one of another (Eph 4:25). From social network communities to the human community" (January 24, 2019).

5. The Vatican opened its first YouTube channel in 2008. Since 2012, the Holy Father has been active on Twitter and since 2016 on Instagram. Parallel to this, the digitally mediated presence of the Pope has become one of the methods of his pastoral engagement, beginning with video messages in the mid-2000s, followed by live video conferencing such as the 2017 meeting with the astronauts of the International Space Station. The Pope's 2017 video message to the Super Bowl in the United States, and his TED Talks in 2017 and 2020 are just two examples of the Pope's digitally mediated pastoral presence.

6. The live broadcast of the March 27, 2020, Statio Orbis drew about 6 million viewers on the Vatican News YouTube Channel and 10 million on Facebook. These numbers do not include later views of the recording of the event or views through other media channels. The same night of the event, 200,000 new followers joined @Franciscus on Instagram, and the posts about March 27, 2020, remain among the most highly engaged content in the history of the account.

7. Among the many Gospel images that could have been chosen as inspiration for this text, the parable of the good Samaritan was chosen, which for Pope Francis is "a parable about communication." Cf. *Message of Pope Francis for the 48th World Communications Day*, "Communication at the Service of an Authentic Culture of Encounter" (January 24, 2014).

8. For example: Who will set the sources from which AI systems learn? Who funds these new producers of public opinion? How can we ensure that those who design the algorithms are guided by ethical principles and help spread globally a new awareness and critical thinking to minimize harm in the new information platforms? New media literacy should cover competencies that not only enable people critically and effectively to engage with information, but also to discern the use of technologies that increasingly reduce the gap between human and nonhuman.

9. Cf. *Fratelli Tutti*, 30; *Evangelii Gaudium*, 220; see also "A Document on Human Fraternity for World Peace and Living Together" (February 4, 2019): "We call upon …

media professionals … in every part of the world to rediscover the values of peace, justice, goodness, beauty, human fraternity, and coexistence in order to confirm the importance of these values as anchors of salvation for all, and to promote them everywhere."

10. "Some people prefer not to ask questions or seek answers; they lead lives of comfort, deaf to the cry of those who suffer. Almost imperceptibly, we grow incapable of feeling compassion for others and for their problems; we have no interest in caring for them, as if their troubles were their own responsibility, and none of our business." *Message of His Holiness Pope Francis for the Celebration of the 49th World Day of Peace*, "Overcome Indifference and Win Peace" (January 1, 2016); *Evangelii Gaudium*, 54.

11. *Message of His Holiness Pope Francis for the Celebration of the 49th World Day of Peace*, "Overcome Indifference and Win Peace" (January 1, 2016).

12. Cf. *Fratelli Tutti*, 67.

13. *Message of His Holiness Pope Francis for the 56th World Day of Social Communications*, "Listening with the Ear of the Heart" (January 24, 2022).

14. *Fratelli Tutti*, 63.

15. "If we are to recognize and focus upon the truly important questions, then silence is a precious commodity that enables us to exercise proper discernment in the face of the surcharge of stimuli and data that we receive." *Message of His Holiness Pope Benedict XVI for the 46th World Communications Day*, "Silence and Word: Path of Evangelization" (January 24, 2012).

16. *Message of Pope Francis for the 48th World Communications Day.*

17. *Message of His Holiness Pope Francis for the 56th World Day of Social Communications*; *Evangelii Gaudium*, 171.

18. "When seeking true communication, the first type of listening to be rediscovered is listening to oneself, to one's truest needs, those inscribed in each person's inmost being. And we can only start by listening to what makes us unique in creation: the desire to be in relationship with others and with the Other." *Message of His Holiness Pope Francis for the 56th World Day of Social Communications.*

19. *Verbum Domini*, 86–87.

20. *Laudato Si'*, 47.

21. Cf. Ibid., 66.

22. *Communio et Progressio*, 12.

23. *Message of Pope Francis for the 53rd World Communications Day.*

24. *Message of Pope Francis for the 48th World Communications Day.*

25. Cf. *Fratelli Tutti*, 49.

26. Ibid., 69.

27. Cf. *Message of Pope Francis for the 48th World Communications Day.*

28. *Fratelli Tutti*, 77.

29. Pope Francis, Angelus, July 10, 2016.

30. Cf. *Gaudete et Exsultate*, 115.

31 On the issue of polarization and its relationship with the building of consensus, see specifically *Fratelli Tutti*, 206–214.

32. Cf. Address at the "Economy of Francesco" event, September 24, 2022.

33. "And the next day he took out two denarii and gave them to the innkeeper, saying, 'Take care of him, and whatever more you spend, I will repay you when I come back'" (Lk 10:35).

34. A survey conducted in the United States by Barna Research Center in 2020 revealed that while half of usual "churchgoers" reported they had not "attended church worship services, either in person or digitally" during a period of six months — they still say

that they have "watched a church service online" during that same period. It is, then, possible to acknowledge having watched a service without counting yourself as an attendee.

35. There seem to be artificial substitutes for almost everything in virtual reality; we can share all kinds of information through digitality, but sharing a meal doesn't seem to be possible even in the metaverse.

36. Cf. *Desiderio Desideravi*, 9, referencing Leo the Great, *Sermo LXXIV: De ascensione Domini II, 1: "quod ... Redemptoris nostri conspicuum fuit, in sacramenta transivit."*

37. *Message of His Holiness Pope Francis for the 53rd World Communications Day*. It may be helpful to consider other forms of spiritual practice, such as the Liturgy of the Hours and *lectio divina*, that might be more suitable for online sharing than the holy Mass.

38. Cf. Pope Francis, *Address to the Plenary Assembly of the Dicastery for Communication*, September 23, 2019.

39. Pope Francis has spoken about God's style as "closeness, compassion, and tenderness" on many occasions (General Audiences, Angelus, Homilies, Press Conferences, etc.).

40. *Communio et Progressio*, 11.

41. "In order to speak well, it is enough to love well" (St. Francis de Sales). Cf. *Message of His Holiness Pope Francis for the 57th World Day of Social Communications*, "Speaking with the heart. The truth in love" (January 24, 2023).

42 *Message of His Holiness Pope Francis for the 52nd World Day of Social Communications*, "The truth will set you free (Jn 8:32). Fake news and journalism for peace" (January 24, 2018).

43. *Message of His Holiness Pope Francis for the 53rd World Day of Social Communications*.

44. It is important though, that when a false narrative emerges, it be corrected respectfully and expeditiously. "Fake news has to be refuted, but individual persons must always be respected, for they believe it often without full awareness or responsibility." *Address of His Holiness Pope Francis to Participants in the Meeting Promoted by the National Consortium of Catholic Media "Catholic Fact-Checking,"* January 28, 2022.

45. *Message of His Holiness Pope Francis for the 50th World Day of Social Communications*, "Communication and mercy: A fruitful encounter" (January 24, 2016).

46. This concerns also the formation of priests. As we read in the Ratio Fundamentalis Institutionis Sacerdotalis, "Pastors of the future cannot be aloof, either during their formation or their future ministry, from the public square of social media" (No. 97). They might be also aware of the inevitable risks that come with frequenting the digital world, including various forms of addiction (cf. No. 99). On this aspect see also the *Address of the Holy Father Pope Francis to Seminarians and Priests Studying in Rome*, October 24, 2022.

47. Cf. *Message of His Holiness Pope Francis for the 53rd World Day of Social Communications*.

48. It might be useful, therefore, that individual initiatives on social media, especially those that originate with religious and clergy, find a way to enhance communion in the Church. As a Christian community, it might be helpful as well to reach out to the "influencers" that are at the margins of our ecclesial environments.

49. Being synodal (from *syn odòs*) means walking on the same road, walking together, moving forward together.

50. This was described by the ancient Church Fathers. Tertullian, for example, spoke about martyrdom as attractiveness. In his Apology, he explains that the persecutions are not only unjust, but also pointless: "None of your cruelty, however exquisite, will avail you; rather, it makes our religion more attractive. The more we are mown down by you, the more we grow in number; the blood of Christians is the seed of a new life. ... That very

obstinacy you rail against is a lesson. For who that contemplates it, is not excited to inquire what is at the bottom of it? Who, after inquiry, does not embrace our doctrines?" Tertullian, *Apology*, chapter 50 (translation adapted).

51. This paragraph is partly inspired by the *Message to the Pontifical Mission Societies*, May 21, 2020.

52. Apostolic Journey to Panama: Vigil with Young People (Campo San Juan Pablo II — Metro Park, January 26, 2019).

53. *Message of Pope Francis for the 48th World Communications Day.*